GREENWICH STYLE

GREENWICH STYLE
Inspired Family Homes

CINDY RINFRET

Principal photography by
Michael Partenio and styled by Stacy Kunstel

RIZZOLI
NEW YORK

All photographs are by Michael Partenio and styled by Stacy Kunstel, with the exception of the following:

Page 27: Nancy Hill

Pages 163–67, 170–83: Emily Minton-Redfield

Pages 168, 169: Kimberly Gavin

Pages 186, 187: Warren Jagger

Pages 202, 203, 212, 213: John Cutler

First published in the United States of America in 2013

by Rizzoli International Publications, Inc.

300 Park Avenue South

New York, NY 10010

www.rizzoliusa.com

2015 2016 2017 / 10 9 8 7 6 5 4 3

Distributed to the U.S. trade by Random House, New York

Design by Subtitle

Printed in China

ISBN-13: 978-0-8478-3954-4

Library of Congress Control Number: 2012950413

INTRODUCTION

The inspiration for all my decorating is family. It doesn't matter if your house is a colonial or contemporary, made from stucco or stone, it simply can't be called a home until it is filled with the lives and experiences of the people who live there.

So it is amazing to me that people still believe they cannot have an elegant, well-designed home that is also a place for family members, children, and pets. I often hear clients say, "Oh, I can't have that because I have a two-year-old" or a slobbery dog. But some of the most inspiring rooms I have created over the years were designed with family living and elegance in mind, including my own home, Laurel Hill, which is as comfortable for my children and my dogs as it is elegant for entertaining.

Our homes are for creating memories. I still remember my first bedroom, which my mother painted in charcoal gray (an odd choice for a child, now that I think about it). The room had bright white furniture, a white iron bed, and billowy white taffeta curtains that I felt looked like Cinderella's ball gown. She decoupaged butterflies all over the walls and then hung more three-dimensional butterflies on clear fishing wire from the ceiling. This was more than just a room; it was my own secret garden, my favorite childhood escape. I love the memory of it even today. My mother was a pretty clever gal, and I think my eye for decorating came from her and that beloved childhood room.

When you create a home, it is not just about furnishing it, but building an environment for you and your family. It should include photographs and collections of the places you have been, along with the pieces of furniture you have acquired over the years or inherited from a favorite relative. A home should contain the odds and ends of life's journeys.

My interiors are places of comfort and security, the kind of spaces you are not afraid to really live in. Every room I design is meant to be used, and not just act as a showpiece for guests. The best compliment I get from a client is, "I actually use my living room. I never did before, except during the holidays." That is exactly the way it should always be.

—Cindy Rinfret

LAUREL HILL
The Designer's Home

One of the great luxuries for any interior design-er is the opportunity to design and build one's own home from the ground up. Such a mean-ingful and personal project presents a unique problem: with all the experience and knowledge you have gained from designing homes for other people over the years, what do you finally design for yourself?

I tackled this potentially overwhelming question by creating a list of things that make me the happiest. At the top of my list was European living. I have always been drawn to the quiet elegance of European country houses. Whenever I return from an overseas trip, I ask myself, "Why can't I have the same feeling for my home back in the States? Why do I have to be on vacation to live this way?"

Also on my list: family, friends, my dogs, and my love for entertaining. I knew that my dream home would need to be a welcoming space for all my loved ones to gather. After all, what is the point of having a fabulous home if you don't plan on sharing it with others?

It was important to me that all members of my family (two legged and otherwise) have access to every room. The "off-limits" dining room or living room would not be a part of my dream home. To keep the house from feeling too precious, I used natural finishes and materials that look better with age. The limestone, stucco, natural wood beams, and distressed floors would complement the understated style I had in mind. In my design studio I grabbed the samples that spoke to this comfortable yet elegant sensibility: linens, leathers, sisal, fur, and simple

I love what I call "inside/outside" decorating. The view of this beautiful garden urn reads like a painting through the French doors and brings the gardens into my home as a glorious background.

fabrics that don't look "decorated."

In my new home I also wanted to bring the outside in. My former home, a classic colonial, was beautiful but had no connection to the landscape. I had to go "visit" my gardens, rather than incorporate them into my home experience. There was a division between what was inside and what was out. For my new home, Laurel Hill, I would blur the line between indoors and outdoors.

To bring my dream home to life, I sought an architect with a shared vision and sensibility. I had admired Jack Arnold's work for many years, and I was confident that he would understand the European sensibility that I envisioned. Jack innately knew what I wanted, and we finalized the design with only six email revisions and two meetings, which is impressive because I am fanatical about getting all the details right before break-

ing ground. I repeatedly advise my clients to take the time upfront to have their projects completely designed down to all the details, from paint finishes to lighting specifications. Then you can sit back and let the professionals do their job.

I also recommend that clients engage an interior designer while still in the early planning stages. The furniture floor plans relate to electric plans and the sizes and locations of your rooms, so it is important to establish your design schemes while there is still time to move walls and change lighting to reflect your floor plan. Making selections for hardware and finishes is much easier when you can visualize your home with the fabrics and colors in mind. The construction, architecture, and interior design all go hand in hand, and it helps if all parties are working in unison from day one.

Outdoor decorating should touch all your senses. The smell of the flowers, the sound of the water from the wall fountain, and the sight of the beautiful grape leaf–covered pergola evoke the feeling of a European courtyard.

The outdoor living room that adjoins the bocce court is everyone's favorite "room" in the house. The sounds of the koi pond fountains and the views of the turtle and fish bring tranquility to this space. My family uses this room even in the winter, when we gather around the blazing fire, wrapped in cozy fur blankets. The candlelit chandelier adds to the ambiance, and we find ourselves telling stories and laughing into the wee hours of the night.

Today Laurel Hill exemplifies to me what family living is all about. Home is a place to gather with your loved ones in a comfortable and relaxed environment. In every room are sentimental pieces that I have collected along my travels around the world. It is a joy to look around and recollect the stories behind so many of my favorite objects.

Good design is in the details. Two of the most important elements for me are hardware and lighting, which immediately dictate the quality of a home. To give my house the feel of a European home, I used chrome bolts on the doors and windows, which add instant continental charm.

Lighting is very important, and it is critical to get the scale right. I always look for light fixtures that are a bit overscaled for the spaces—I dislike when a light fixture is dwarfed by the room. I also don't like when a light fixture lacks any kind of character or age. For my kitchen I installed large lanterns over the island and added sconces behind the stove. The kitchen opens into the family room, and the lighting makes it feel like a part of the living space.

This house was geared around outdoor entertaining. I came up with a design that placed garden courtyards outside all the windows. The entire home has long French doors to make the outside easily accessible to the inside. The house was designed as part of the landscape—one complete thought. From my bedroom I now have direct access (via French doors) to my koi pond, gardens, and terrace. I often take my coffee from the bedroom into the

To reach the breakfast room you must travel down what I call a "connector space"— a romantic hall that is lit by a row of stunning light fixtures. The only decoration in this hall is a fantastic iron console and gorgeous mirror, which I was lucky to find on one of my antiquing adventures. Windows and doors in this hall look out to my beloved gardens.

A butler's pantry is essential to a good kitchen. It allows a caterer to keep the mess out of your kitchen when you are entertaining. A pantry also doubles as a potting room for creating flower arrangements and feeding your orchids. And it is a wonderful space to house your specialty dishes and glasses, while keeping them close to your kitchen. I believe you should use your wonderful dishes and accessories every day, not just on special occasions. Every day should be special, and you should set your table with style and beauty. Always have flowers, linen napkins, and lit hurricane lamps.

I love to bring an element of surprise and sense of humor into a home. I created a secret door from the library to the upstairs children's quarters. As a child I was always enchanted by secret passages, so I designed a door from a library shelf (complete with faux leather-bound books) that slides away to create access to the floor above.

The design of the house allows for every window to have a view of a courtyard. Everyone loves cuddling up on a cozy window seat overlooking this beautifully landscaped yard.

gardens for a calming moment before starting the day. From the library there is a gorgeous view of the outdoor living room. To the right of the library, grand French doors frame my "golden retriever rose garden," which is marked by my two stone dog statues—a tribute to my dog family. My beloved golden retriever Sconset is buried beneath one of the statues, and I smile when I remember her spirit.

The decoration inside my home is influenced by the outdoors. In the family room I installed outdoor lanterns over the doors. One would typically use these fixtures outside, but their soft light makes for a gracious atmosphere that looks beautiful against my wood beamed ceilings. I even used planked shutters in my rustic mudroom, lending the space a casual yet elegant air.

The outside world is also brought inside through the sounds and smells that filter into the home: the water dripping into the fountain pool, the leaves rustling in the breeze, and the fragrance of a fresh spring garden. Windows and doors are kept open as often as possible.

Never underestimate the powder room—all your guests will see it. For my powder room I found an amazing antique door in Tuscany and built the entire concept of the room around it. To complete the old-world look I installed antique reclaimed terra-cotta floors that look as if they belong in Tuscany. While shopping at Treillage in New York City, I found a fountain that once had a cistern. I took the piece apart, lined the top with copper, and added a copper sink. The result is this jewel of a sink. There is a beautifully carved chair rail and upholstered walls in a deer moiré that I finished off with a simple linen gimp.

This vignette (above) is a testament to mixing things you love. The console is Italian, the urn is from Thailand, the suede chairs are English, and the sketches are from Florence. The lovely stag mirrors are reproductions from Bedford, Massachusetts. Design is about the use of scale and texture, and living with things that you love.

I love finding antique pieces to set sinks into. For the mudroom bathroom (opposite) I found an antique bamboo chest. I carried the bamboo detail into the chair rail and upholstered the walls in English linen. The room has a very French feel thanks to a collection of framed eighteenth-century bird prints and a mirror made to fit the space. Guests always comment on how lovely this cozy, detailed space is.

The headboard in my master bedroom was discovered during a cab ride in Chang Mai, Thailand, in a section of town where salvaged artifacts from torn-down buildings and temples are sold along the road. The Thai people respect the past and use reclaimed pieces as often as possible. The past offers significant spiritual importance and so the older the object, the more cherished it becomes. I instinctively knew that this temple relic would fit beautifully on the wall of my bedroom. I had a vision of adding to it a gorgeous antique velvet backing that would transform it into the most unique headboard. My wood relic had to be cut into three pieces before we could ship it to Connecticut. Today it reminds me of how the travels of an inanimate object can be so powerfully transforming.

The master bath was created not only as a tranquil quiet retreat but as a place to contemplate the beauty of good design. The Gracie paper on the walls was custom painted in a calming scene of branches and flowers in a neutral color palette. It has a timeless quality that again brings the outdoor element inside. This space melts all the worries of the day away.

Entertaining is always important when you have children, as you want them to prefer being home to being out. Our home is the gathering place for my teen children and their friends. We have a "teen disco" on the lower level with a French bistro vibe. I have had more than a few great dinner parties down in the bistro myself.

CLASSIC CONNECTICUT
A Family Estate in Greenwich

I always say a decorator is only as good as her client. By this, I mean that the collaboration between both client and designer should be based on a shared level of respect and vision. It also helps when clients know what they want and put together an all-star team to achieve it. For this project I had the privilege to work with the premier architect Dinyar Wadia and a visionary and detail-oriented builder, Sound Beach Partners. It was a true team effort with a winning result.

The immediate challenge was that we were tasked with designing, building, landscaping, decorating, accessorizing, and installing an expansive limestone estate with a pool and a seemingly countless number of rooms from start to finish in just eighteen months.

The clients wanted to build a home that would be in keeping with the other houses on the established street where they had purchased their property. Their limestone and slate-roof mansion, now completed, feels as if it has always been in the neighborhood. The finished house is truly an estate, complete with pool, tennis courts, and sweeping porches. However, the interiors are understated and meant to be enjoyed and lived in with friends, children, and even the golden retriever.

The entry offered a challenge: with its grand thirty-foot ceilings, how could this space offer a warm and inviting introduction to the house? To balance the scale, I chose jumbo lanterns from Charles Edwards in London that could hold their own in the space. The magnificent Chippendale railing designed by Dinyar Wadia inspired my design elsewhere in the house. An entry of this size requires a large table, and I chose one that could double as an extra dining table or gathering space for parties. The entry rug is important, as it is the first impression of the house. My client and I had a lot of fun selecting the perfect colors to include in this custom rug, which I had made in Bhutan by the rug dealer JD Staron.

The jumping-off point for the living room design were the three beautiful rugs that define the sitting areas. The subtle mix of tones in these rugs inspired the colors for the rest of the room. The plaster ceiling is breathtaking in its detail, so we painted it cream and blue to accentuate the details of the plaster relief work. A gray rock crystal chandelier grabs your eye like a stunning piece of jewelry and draws your attention up to the elaborate ceiling (previous pages). The ceiling and rugs in this space are so magnificent that the furnishings and accessories had to be elegantly restrained. I designed blue textured walls to highlight the embroidered linen curtains hung on metal rings and wood poles. Some of these poles were custom made to fit the curve of the windowed alcoves. I did not want to hide the beautiful transoms and the gracious height of the doors and windows, so the window treatments are understated yet beautifully detailed.

The living room subtly mixes linens and shagreen, velvet and needlepoint. Every place you turn is another interesting detail, like the nail heads on an ottoman or a mirrored side table. Nothing fights for attention in this room. All these elements work together to create an inviting and livable space.

The dining room is a truly inspired mix of ideas. I had the vision to create a mirrored Chippendale chair rail that would relate to the beautiful Chippendale entry railing but with a more updated, transitional feel. Sound Beach Partners brilliantly brought this vision to reality and installed mirror behind the wainscoting. For the walls I chose a traditional damask pattern from Farrow and Ball, which offsets the elegantly detailed curtains that were made from a blue wool accented with embroidered Colfax & Fowler fabric along the border. The design and quiet detail of this border inspired the pattern of the custom rug that we had JD Staron create for this room.

I used two chandeliers in wood and matte crystals. I always feel that two chandeliers seem more understated than one dominant chandelier in a large dining room. We chose a casual plank table, and instead of traditional dining chairs, I installed comfortable upholstered chairs that carry the embroidered details from the curtain borders. Mixing chair styles, as we did here with the head chairs and alcove seating, makes the room feel more collected and authentic. Accessories like a pagoda, mercury glass vases, and blue and white porcelain lend a transitional element to the dining room, which is great for both formal and informal entertaining.

The library is far more than just a place to read. It has a flat-screen TV, a great fireplace, lounge spaces, and an inviting alcove that offers the perfect spot to open your laptop and work from home. Crocodile walls and suede ceilings are mixed with blue and brown wool curtains edged in suede, as well as mohair in the sofa and horsehair in the fireplace fender. Lanterns were custom stained to match the wood paneling. The eclectic feel in this library comes from the mix of furnishings, such as the stag-horn coffee table that rests upon a classic, custom-colored rug from Bhutan.

I have a thing for connector spaces, as they bring together the entire design of a home. The main-floor hallway is especially spectacular with its colonnade of iron lanterns, elegant benches for seating, and textured linen and velvet curtains that add warmth to the space.

When you have a brood of children and lots of friends and family, you need a kitchen that allows you to entertain, do homework, and prepare holiday meals or just everyday family dinners. This kitchen does it all. The cabinets are painted in a silvery cream, which is accented by a slate gray blue at the base of the kitchen island and behind the glass cabinets. I designed the kitchen island to feel more like a piece of furniture: it has silver travertine for the countertops and wood for the base. I tweaked the ordinary by adding brass bolts to the stainless-steel hood. Large lanterns make the scale of the room feel more intimate.

This charming breakfast room makes a statement with a custom birdcage table and a chandelier with smoke-colored hurricane shades. A tongue and groove–paneled ceiling adds texture and detail to this uniquely shaped room. In the bay we created a nook with a curved banquette that is perfect for a cup of tea. I also installed a stone table for lounging and reading the paper. My clients enjoy casual meals in this breakfast room every day.

The magnificent limestone trumeau mantel in the family room may command your attention, but the details in this room really impress. The beautifully hand-stitched and appliquéd curtains, custom made by Holland and Sherry, define the gracious French doors so that they are balanced with the grand mantel and play up the symmetry of the architecture. The blending of the blue and cream in the curtain embroidery synthesizes the entire room's color scheme into one simple design. It is remarkable the effect that a detail like embroidered curtains can have on such a large room.

A comfortable sectional with double chaises offers plenty of seating, and a leather ottoman on casters can conveniently turn to accommodate TV viewing from all angles of the room. A game table works just as well for homework as it does for backgammon. Even the family's golden retriever likes to sneak onto the chaise by the fire after a long day of being chased by the children.

The master suite encompasses a sitting room, a bedroom that opens to porches, his-and-her baths, and dressing rooms. Luxurious textures and a quiet palette of cream and blue make for a soothing environment. The three-dimensional design of this neutral rug with textured needlework highlights the stunning plaster relief ceiling (previous pages). The tufted bed and impressive architecture are elegant and beautiful, yet the mood is made young and fresh by a modern hand-blown glass chandelier.

In the master bathroom are stunning marble floors that go from polished to matte, and a round tub that wraps around the bay windows (opposite). Motorized sheers surround the bath for privacy but also add an ethereal romance to the space. I found a chaise with elegant lines and had it covered in a luxurious cream terry cloth for fun and functionality. An art deco dressing table that feels very old Hollywood was installed in the window along with a whimsical heart-shaped chair, which I again upholstered in the soft terrycloth (above).

Each of the three children's bedrooms is as unique as the child who sleeps there. The sons' room (previous pages) feels very all-American with its red, white, and blue color scheme. Details like suede and nail head on the windows give the room a masculine tone that will still feel appropriate as he grows older. We chose a day bed that can be used for studying or for a sleepover.

The younger daughter loved the calming palette of tan and teal blue (above). In her bedroom she has a beautiful window seat that is set into a round alcove. There's even room in there for extra storage. She also has a comfortable chaise where she can relax with a good book.

The eldest daughter had a more daring color scheme in mind: aqua and purple (following pages). I took the modern glam look she wanted into the ceiling, which is papered in a pattern of silver and soft purple. It is reminiscent of the plaster relief ceilings elsewhere in the house but with a funky edge. On either side of the sleek four-poster bed are mirrored tables that add some bling. The sitting area has touches of purple in throw pillows and in a studded garden stool. This room has a classic yet fresh feel that is perfect for a teenage girl.

TRANSITIONAL COLONIAL
A Classic Connecticut Home with an Asian Flair

I was brought into this project in the very early stages to help bring together the divergent ideas of this couple: the modern, transitional style preferred by the wife, with the more conservative taste of her husband. I was happy to have the opportunity to work with the well-respected Greenwich architectural firm Hilton-Vanderhorn, which designed an iconic Connecticut estate for this couple, their two children, and their beautiful whippet dog.

The couple wanted to honor the husband's Asian heritage and highlight their impressive collection of antique Asian artwork and furniture. The challenge was to give the house the sophistication and luxury that the husband wanted as well as the more transitional look that the wife loved, all while making this home function for the lifestyle of a young, active family. To achieve these grand goals, I focused on three elements that were carried throughout the house: Asian artifacts, a soothing blue and cream color scheme, and Greek key motifs.

I used the clients' phenomenal collection of Asian artifacts throughout the design, which added personality and intrigue to the interiors. They let me use my imagination with their collection and allowed me to create beautiful custom pieces from their antiques. I made

The Greek key theme appears in the curtains, which were custom made by Holland and Sherry from luxurious blue wool with appliquéd Greek key in chocolate velvet along the leading edge. A fabulous Asian chest was mixed with antique porcelain vases and Chinese prints, set against a woven chevron grass-cloth wall covering in soft tans and blues by Phillip Jeffries. The eclectic blend of modern and ancient in the entry dictated the design of the entire home.

a headboard for their master bedroom out of an ancient wood screen and created mirrors out of Asian artifacts.

Both the husband and wife wanted a peaceful color palette for their home, so we selected a soothing blend of soft blues, browns, and ivory. I chose finishes and accents in satin nickel and crystal to add a transitional influence to the design. Using satin nickel can give a modern edge to pieces that would otherwise feel more traditional. It was a great way to appeal to the wife's modern tastes while keeping the traditional lines that the husband preferred.

The Greek key design can also feel modern or transitional, depending on the context. Greek key can be found all around the house, such as in the embroidery on window treatments, in the nail head detail on the master bedroom headboard, in a throw pillow border, and in the design of a mirror. Even the architecture of the house paid tribute to the client's love for Greek key: the living room mantel molding is Greek key, as is the crown molding, and even the library paneling has a Greek key design, not to mention the inlaid marble floor in the master bath.

By listening to the clients and taking inspiration from their own collections, I created interiors that translated their family's histories, loves, and travels into a place that they can both call their dream home.

The custom-painted chinoiserie wall covering by De Gournay in the untraditional color palette of blues, grays, brown, and silver gives a subtle Asian influence to the dining room. Anchoring this room is a rock crystal chandelier by Holly Hunt with a smoky patina that looks beautiful against the silvery blue walls. A gong from the client's antique collection makes for a magnificent accent in the window (and is also a fun way to ring guests to dinner). The curtains are a mix of velvet and textured linen.

The living room pays tribute to our love for Greek key, which can be found in the coffee table legs, mirror, and pillows. These pieces are paired with seating upholstered in luxurious chenille and velvet fabrics. The wing chairs are a traditional choice but have a modern edge thanks to nickel nail head detail. The Nierman Weeks beaded chandelier is paired with mercury sconces that frame the mantel.

The kitchen was designed by my go-to kitchen designer, Christopher Peacock, who is a master at creating classic English scullery, but with all the best modern conveniences. I love the classic scullery details like the butcher board and walnut beadboard in the back of the cabinets. We accented the room with a blue ceiling and modern Vaughn light fixtures that have linen shades. The accessories and lighting, like a classic hurricane lantern, have a polished nickel finish that instantly transforms their traditional design into something transitional.

The butler's pantry (above) is based in tradition but has a stainless-steel countertop and an amazing blue tortoiseshell backsplash.

The breakfast room (opposite) is an architectural gem, with an octagonal shape, French doors and windows, a beautifully detailed ceiling, and an intricate pattern in the antique floor boards. A glamorous mercury glass chandelier anchors the room, and the breakfast table with a stone base and planked walnut top bring an indoor/outdoor element. I love using outdoor furniture indoors for an unexpected twist, especially in a room like this one, which has such spectacular views to the expansive lawn. The chairs were upholstered in a fabric that brings together the colors in the table, walls, and chandelier.

The color palette in the family room (above) is reversed, with tan walls, modern horizontal stripe curtains, and eucalyptus leaf prints set in mercury frames. I love the tight needlework rug with the blue and cocoa chinoiserie pattern, as it completely pulls this room together.

Mixing old and new, and combining textures of shiny and matte, give a room style and confidence. I love the mercury glass vases against the woven grass cloth. The unexpected use of colors and materials keeps a room from looking ordinary.

The master bedroom captures the personalities of my clients beautifully (previous pages). The palette is celadon, tan, and ivory. The headboard was custom made from an antique Asian screen that my client had discovered. I attached the screen against a velvet upholstered board and added Greek key detail along the perimeter to lengthen the piece to accommodate a king bed. On either side of the bed are deco antique mirror tables with gold tea paper gourd lamps. The curtains are tan silk with vertical stripe Greek key embroidery in celadon, with a pole detail and Greek key finials in silver leaf. They work beautifully against the tan and celadon wool and silk combed rug. My client's existing corner chairs (above) and a beautifully hand-carved screen look perfect in front of the fireplace, which I accented with a unique chevron tile insert.

The design of the master bath (opposite) started with the inlay marble Greek key floor border. We designed the vanities and bathtub surround to reflect this detail and to bring light into the room. The Greek key details extend to the silver leaf and antique mirror cornice, which also evokes the design in the master headboard. There is a translucent shade that comes down from the cornice when privacy is needed. We added modern pieces like freestanding crystal sinks that pair beautifully with custom mirrored vanities. A cherry blossom wall covering by Kravet makes the walls feel like a scene from a Japanese cherry blossom festival.

This bath even has a sitting area, where one can pause to take in the peaceful environment. I was able to incorporate the client's existing wing chairs but updated them with a modern fabric. The addition of beaded throw pillows transformed these old chairs into something new and fresh.

My client requested a room her daughter could grow into but that would still speak to her young, feminine personality. We found a silver gray and purple fabric with shocking pink accents and paired it with a silk fabric inset with mirrors to create the canopy bed. We mixed Lucite, iron, mirrored tables, and a shell chandelier for added glamour. For her bath we added a window seat with mirrored drawers and glass tiles that look almost like mother-of-pearl bricks in the tub.

For the son we wanted a masculine British Colonial space that would appeal to his curious young mind. His cherished collection of books became the focal point of this room, with a grand bookshelf that spanned an entire wall and framed his bed. The upholstered headboard in suede is accented with nail heads and lends a contemporary edge to the bookshelf. A favorite fabric of mine from Pierre Frey of old world maps, paired with a British Colonial desk, continues the idea of exotic adventure and exploration.

This library has a bar, billiard table, and spiral staircase down to the wine cellar. The walnut paneling brings a warm tone, which is more inviting than the imposing dark walls in a traditional mahogany library. Touches of animal skin in the bar stool and billiard chairs add some fun to this masculine space.

FRENCH COUNTRY ESTATE
A Family Manor

This home inspires you to believe that you can have it all: beautiful interiors in a home that functions for the daily life of an energetic brood.

I had decorated the client's previous home, and part of this project was integrating all the pieces that she had collected and loved into this new, much larger residence, which had beautiful proportions. We had an existing palette of neutrals and soft blues from the interiors of her previous home, so we built upon that color scheme for the design of the new house.

The house has a wonderful pool and cabana with an outdoor fireplace and tennis court. Outdoor spaces are just as important as indoor spaces and extend your home for entertaining and lounging. Down the hill we created a secret garden with a gazebo and a frog pond. The children are entertained for hours here.

This home is designed for both entertaining and the lifestyle of an active family. No room is off limits. Every inch of this home is used and loved on a daily basis.

The entry foyer greets you with a handsome console covered with blue and white porcelain and a bull's-eye mirror set against custom strié wallpaper. The wall covering and unique light fixtures continue through the hallways and bring a cohesive design element to the house. The large hurricane candle sconces are gorgeous when lit for dinner parties.

The foyer opens to a perfectly square dining room with an antique dining table and an eighteenth-century crystal chandelier. The mix of the hand-painted Gracie wall covering against unadorned windows makes the room feel fresh and young and shows off the beautiful doors and hardware. Pops of red chinoiserie accents add interest to the room.

The living room has beautiful transom openings to the dining room (opposite). The neutral-colored upholstery is accented by geometric Greek key pillows to create a modern yet classic look. The walls are treated with an unusual grass cloth that has gold leaf woven into the background—a detail that makes the room subtly shimmer. Although the furnishings are more traditional, the wall covering and accessories give the room a more transitional feel.

Off the living room is a beautiful walnut library (following pages). We mixed sisal and zebra skin with stag furniture and suede chairs to give the room an eclectic, collected feel.

The sitting room was originally painted a striking aubergine color (opposite). The client and I both found it unexpected and exciting, so we decided to design the room around this bold color. Interestingly enough, the client had the perfect rug and artwork. I designed a unique banquette with an intricate nail-head design and found two garden stools that pulled the entire concept together. We added a chinoiserie paper to the barrel-vaulted ceiling that makes the room feel finished and inviting.

In the client's previous home we had designed a kitchen with fabulous natural-colored bamboo cabinetry. Leaving behind that kitchen, which had just been completed, was the one big compromise in moving. As beautiful as this new home was, the kitchen was dull and boring with depressing, dark cabinetry. My client wanted to rip the kitchen out and start again, but with children, a complete kitchen renovation can be a logistical nightmare. I came to her with the idea of rebuilding all the exterior doors and painting the island instead (above). This way the kitchen was minimally disturbed, as most of the woodwork could be done in the shop and installed on site. I added the bamboo details she loved to all the doors and created new panels that made the refrigerator look like an armoire with an antique mirror. The granite countertops remained the same, but we painted all the cabinets a parchment color and I had a faux painter darken all the bamboo detail to look real. The lighter color of the cabinets, in conjunction with the antique mirror accents, completely brightened up any dark shadows that had previously lurked in this kitchen. Last, we updated the faucets and lighting and succeeded in completely transforming this dark, drab kitchen to a light, airy space that everyone loves to be in.

Off the kitchen is a breakfast bay that the children had coopted for their projects. But there was no storage, and my client was exasperated by the clutter. The solution became a cabinet I designed with mirrored panels that continued the bamboo molding detail from the kitchen. It offered a place to store the children's art supplies and completed the window detail around the room, which had the added benefit of making the space seem more symmetrical. I found a stain-resistant chinoiserie fabric for the chairs, and now the breakfast room is as functional as it is beautiful.

The house has a beautiful pool and cabana (following pages), and we created a secret garden and gazebo with frog pond. The twig furniture is concrete and can be kept out all year long.

Dressing rooms and baths are the first places you go in the morning and should give you a happy start to the day. I like to treat all rooms as rooms, not just functional places. It is nice to have a comfortable place to sit while putting on your shoes or looking through your closet. Start your day off in style.

TRANSITIONAL STYLE
A Former Show House Becomes a Family Home

It is hard to believe that this classic Greenwich stone house that so beautifully accommodates the lifestyle of a young, active family was once a disjointed decorator show house. Each room had a different theme and vision, and I give a lot of credit to my client for seeing that the house had great bones, in spite of the distracting decorating schemes. It was my job to transform these showy rooms into a cohesive design.

I had previously designed two homes for the family, and for this project, my client wanted to make a traditional house feel younger. To achieve this, I gave classic pieces a modern twist. The look is a bit unconventional for a grand Greenwich home, but it works because it enhances the intrinsic elegance and grace of the architecture. Although my client had strong ideas on the direction of the design, she was open to letting me recalibrate her idea of how the family would use this house. Every detail was chosen with the goal of providing a place for the family to enjoy their time together and create memories for years to come.

The first impression of this house is the standard entry, which had a classic black and white floor. To tone the traditional element down, we added a custom wool diamond-patterned sisal rug.

The living room in this house is enormous at almost forty feet long. Three large walnut lanterns helped to fill out the grand ceiling and transformed the room from intimidating to inviting. The focus of the room is the limestone mantel with stainless-steel surround. Wing chairs with modern lines frame the mantel for a look that is grounded in tradition but a lot more fun. The relaxed mood of the room is also reflected in the suede throw pillows with inset tape and the Holland & Sherry blue wool window panels on nickel rings in front of bamboo blinds. This mix of casual fabrics, modern materials, and inviting furniture pieces creates a room that is instantly approachable and begs to be lived in.

We anchored this grand space with a modern console flanked by corner chairs (above). Large urns balance the scale of the landing and play off the clean lines of the console. Hodsoll McKenzie curtains with pale blue sheers make for a glamorous sight from the first floor.

What do you do with a forty-foot living room? This client did not want a living room you just pass by but one her family would actually use. So we used her billiard table at one end and added a bar with TV at the other. This guaranteed people would come in and enjoy this beautiful room.

The fireplace is a classic with a twist. We inserted an unexpected brushed-stainless-steel surround into this limestone mantel, which works beautifully and makes the room more transitional. It also balances the églomisé mirror above and the unexpected nickel nail heads on a more modern wing chair—all classic ideas with a fresh, new look.

Adjoining the living room is a sunroom with a large stone fireplace (opposite). We added a herringbone tongue-and-groove ceiling to create a casual feel and to bring down the height of the twelve-foot ceilings so the room would feel more intimate. The room felt exposed in the winter months, and the trellis-patterned linen curtains on simple iron poles make it cozier. Like the window treatments, all the fabrics for the furniture are linen, and the rugs are sisal and wool. I accessorized with garden elements to add interest to the space.

The breakfast room (above) works beautifully for family gatherings or just day-to-day meals. Again, I added the tongue-and-groove paneling to the ceiling to give it some charm and character. The walls were installed with a blue and tan woven raffia wall covering that lends the space a relaxed feel. The windows surrounding the room have simple side panels on iron poles in printed linen, which offer a very cozy, homespun feel; yet the modern fabric design gives a touch of the unexpected. We call the table the "birdcage" table because of its unique base. Simple chairs were upholstered in blue woven fabric with nail heads, and accessories include mercury glass vases and baskets.

The client requested a blue, tan, and brown color scheme thoughout the home, and we brought these colors into the dining room (opposite) with a matte De Gournay silk wall covering and painted the wainscot a limestone color to play off the fireplaces throughout the home. The client had a beautiful antique table and traditional chairs, which we gave new life by reupholstering in blue velvet backs and a tan and blue velvet stripe front. A pair of chandeliers in matte crystal with bleached and glazed wood and iron balances the more formal crystal deco sconces that my client had. The rug was custom colored in this gorgeous interlocking trellis design.

I energized the client's existing antique entry table (above) by adding two benches upholstered in a relaxed raffia with nickel nail head. This mix of the traditional and new sets the tone for a transitional interior. The twig lanterns from Holly Hunt are classic in shape but a little less formal than expected, which is exactly what we wanted for this space.

The kitchen underwent the biggest transformation in the house. The original kitchen had formal dark wood cabinets, but my client wanted a fresh, younger feel, so the decision was made to go with an old-world concept of a scullery kitchen, treated in a modern way with stainless-steel counters and appliances. We collaborated with the master of the scullery kitchen, Christopher Peacock, on this design overhaul. For the backsplash we used classic Carrera marble cut into narrow bricks. The hood over the stove was custom made from glass and stainless steel. To pull it all together I selected a modern geometric light fixture. The finished product is fresh, modern, and anything but stuffy.

Unexpected pieces like a unique tray sink and an elaborate carved mirror in the powder room are set off against luxe upholstered walls (above). The lighting is an eclectic combination of deco sconces and a modern hanging light fixture in nickel.

The family room had a wonderful geometric ceiling that we complemented with a zinc chandelier from the client's previous home (opposite). We mounted the TV over the fireplace because windows and doors surrounded the room. The purpose here was to create a lounge space where the children could gather with their friends. The room is a sand color with accents of blue on the pillows, plus faux fur and chenille accessories.

The master suite was all about creating a glamorous and romantic sanctuary (previous pages). We set the mood with modern glam statement pieces—like mirrored bedside tables and a striking glass chandelier—to add sparkle to the silvery blue color scheme. The beauty of this room is in the details: custom designed cornices for the curtains that somehow feel both traditional and modern, mirror accents in the half-canopy bed, and luxurious materials everywhere. We grounded the room with a soft, silky carpet. In the sitting area, the romance continues in the form of cashmere throws and mercury glass lamps (above).

The old-world glamour of the master suite continues to her bathroom (opposite), which features a custom-designed vanity, crystal chandelier, and a traditional floral wall covering in matte silver and tan. The tiles are polished and honed in a classic basket weave design. The tub is freestanding in front of the window, which gives it a very sculptural feel.

In the gentleman's bath are Denby marble floors, which bring in tan, gray, and beige colors that are softer and warmer than the classic choice of Carrera marble. A custom walnut vanity works beautifully against the flooring. Another knockout piece is the nickel-faced steeping tub with an iron bench. Curtains in a wool plaid fabric in blue and cream evoke men's suiting. We added textured woven shades throughout the bath for privacy but also to give a warmer, more casual feel to the space.

The master dressing room (above) has custom built-ins in light walnut. I designed a roman shade in the same wool plaid fabric from the bath. It was wonderful to discover that two beautiful leather chairs from the client's previous home looked perfect in this space.

The teenage son wanted a room that he would still love to return to once he went to college. I designed for him a very masculine room with a leather tufted bed and chair, linen curtains banded in suede, and a transitional light fixture. It's simple, tailored, and elegant.

The daughter's room has dormered ceilings so we created a sitting room perfect for reading and studying but also for sleepovers. My client's daughter wanted a modern blue and white scheme so I chose a linen paisley fabric with an almost Moroccan vibe. We installed a white leather upholstered bed with nickel nail head, flanked by swing-arm lamps. Shoe prints in silver frames completed the feminine and fun look.

We completely started from scratch for the daughter's bathroom, using white tile with a vessel sink and mirrored vanity. Additional storage space was created with a bench upholstered in white terry cloth.

When you have a home of significant size, what do you do with all that extra space? We made this house into a country club unto itself. In the basement there is a complete gym, as well as a lacrosse field and half-basketball court.

On the third floor is a spacious home theater that comfortably seats twenty.

Outside there are grand terraces for enjoying the outdoor kitchen with pizza oven. A fire pit offers a fantastic gathering spot on a chilly night.

CLASSIC SHINGLE STYLE
A House at the Water's Edge

I was in the midst of installing a home during a tremendous snowstorm in Vail when I received a frantic phone call from a Californian couple visiting Connecticut. They had just bought a house on the water and needed to see me immediately. I explained to them that this might be difficult, as most of the highways in Vail had been closed due to the snow. Luckily, they postponed their departure back to California and the snow in Colorado finally let up, so I was able to get to Connecticut in time to meet these potential clients and see their new acquisition.

The couple had purchased a shingle-style home on the water in a lovely beachside community near Greenwich called Wilson Point. They explained that their grown children and grandchildren were all now on the East Coast, and they needed to make a home here that could accommodate their expanding brood. The objective was to create an oasis from the city for their children and grandchildren to come visit.

The wife had a strong vision of what she wanted and she found it on this secluded marshland peninsula. The idyllic property came with its own dock that gives direct

For the living room I had JD Staron, one of my favorite rug designers, reproduce a design for me in Bhutan. With its gorgeous color scheme of celadon, greens, tans, and warm browns, this rug became the inspiration for the design of the living room. To complement the colors in the rug we stained the floors a light walnut that immediately gave the room the warmth and richness that it needed. To complete the newly designed room, the homeowners found a beautiful painting of their own coastline view at a local gallery, and we hung it over the mantel. The paint colors worked seamlessly with the scheme of the room, and this artwork made for the perfect focal point.

access to the water. The client had the enchanting idea to create a Shakespearean garden connecting the home to the dock, which came to life beautifully under the direction of landscape architect Tara Vincenta.

The interior design of the house was of utmost importance to my client, as she longed to have a warm and inviting living space that would complement the classic shingle-style architecture. The existing design of the interiors was dated and had a modern edge to it that was not in keeping with her idea of a welcoming home. She and her husband wanted an understated, comfortable living environment that would feel like part of the landscape.

There were a number of architectural elements to deal with in this house. The floors were pickled to a very pink/mauve color that must have fallen out of fashion twenty years earlier. Cabinetry and postmodern architectural columns divided the living areas into awkward spaces. Sometimes it is not what you put into a house but what you take out that makes all the difference. This was certainly the case in this project.

I cleaned up the rooms by ripping out the dated cabinetry and left clean, open spaces. Even in the construction phase, this simple change suddenly created a flow from one room to the next, which completely opened up the first floor. We kept French doors, which opened to what would become an amazing view of the gardens. The

---

The existing living room fireplace was cumbersome with its built-in bookshelves that felt dated and made the room feel smaller. I had the bookshelves removed, which instantly lengthened the space, and installed a simple limestone mantel (opposite). Wrought-iron planters overflowing with hydrangea filled the spaces where the bookshelves had once been. Ripping out these bookshelves also revealed the slight barrel ceiling— a wonderful and subtle detail that had been obscured by the cabinetry.

To make this room feel more intimate I installed an elegant sofa, deep upholstered chairs, and two unique wood-frame armchairs with carved lion-head details (following pages). I rounded out the room with a pair of small ottomans, which can function as seating but also give focus to the mantel. Behind the ottomans is a simple iron and glass coffee table that lets the beauty of the rug show through and gives this small space room to breathe. Curtains were constructed from a woven silk and linen fabric and are accented with a contrast banding and woven tape.

idea was to bring the outside in, as the client had plans to add a pool, terraces, an outdoor kitchen, and a gazebo that she wanted to see from the house.

The decoration of the home began with my very first purchase for this client, a unique wrought-iron and stone armillary sundial. There was a curved bay in the dining room that really needed a focal point and this was it. I found this garden ornament while shopping for antiques soon after I received the signed contract. It was constructed from various antique architectural elements: the fluted base is made from an 1870s New York City street pedestal and the stone neck is an Italian urn fragment.

From this outstanding piece, I drew inspiration for the rest of the home. I brought the client's love of her gardens inside the house with garden ornaments and continued the soothing palette of the landscape indoors with a color scheme of sage, linen, and browns that reflected the marshland, grasses, and surrounding cove.

This home is the ultimate family getaway, as it is not only an oasis for my clients but a virtual fantasyland for their children and grandchildren. The combined effect of the Shakespearean gardens, the views of the Long Island Sound, the welcoming interiors, and the owners' wonderful spirit make it a very special place.

I drew inspiration for the design of this home from the unique wrought-iron and stone armillary sundial that is now in the curved bay of the dining room.

The family room had a dark, low ceiling, so we whitewashed the beams to elevate the height of the room (following pages). I chose subtle colors of brown, khaki, and beige in the furniture to complement the linen curtains. These colors blend very well with the large stone mantel to create one cohesive space. All the chairs in this room swivel to face the television, and a large leather ottoman adds a relaxed feel.

We worked with the existing cabinets in the kitchen and added light and space to the room with antique mirrored doors (opposite). A new pantry storage area with screening and metal grillwork added texture and interest to the space. There's a charming window alcove in the family room (above) that we made into a little dining spot with a breakfast table and two chairs with nail-head detail beneath an iron lantern. It is a wonderful place to sit and have lunch while looking out to the view of the pool and terraces beyond.

The master bedroom has soaring ceilings with beams that we had painted. I installed a very large iron-leaf chandelier to bring the scale of the ceiling down to canopy height. The iron-and-wood canopy bed has a custom-designed TV unit at the foot that goes up or down at the touch of a button. I also designed a vanity area (above) that could double as a writing table. Each drawer is fitted for jewelry and has additional storage space for stationery.

The master bathroom (opposite) was the biggest challenge in this house. We gutted two small, cramped bathrooms to create one spacious bath with two large vanities with custom cabinetry and mirror details that are balanced by the tub. The stone is cream and pale green and the walls are covered in gray-green vinyl raffia. The space sparkles and reflects like the water views outside.

The magnificent round seating area in the master bedroom (above) has motorized shades to close the curtains and sheers. I designed an octagonal ottoman for relaxation.

Off the kitchen is an elegant private office with a lovely chaise (above). We created beautiful and functional built-in cabinetry to accommodate the computer, printers, and other office needs. An upholstered ribbon memo board keeps invitations, family photos, and reminders organized. The cotton reversible rug is from Elizabeth Eakins.

This bedroom had a unique architectural element of a round bay and a vaulted ceiling (opposite). I found an iron bed that fit into this alcove perfectly and made a powerful impact in this small room. The design of the room reinforces the garden theme with a chocolate brown and cream trellis design in the rug, and aged stone urn lamps on the bedside tables. The brown and green color scheme in the bedding and rug is continued in the gorgeous embroidered curtains and sheers that frame the bed.

This bathroom (above) was designed with walnut cabinetry and crisp Carrera and Emperador marble tile. The brown and white embroidered shower curtain is clean and elegant.

The weekend guest suite (opposite) has a transitional mix of furnishings, including this comfortable seating area.

CONTEMPORARY MOUNTAIN HOME
A House for an Active Family

For this project I was tasked with designing a contemporary house with stunning views of the mountain on a property that had the distinction of being the last ski-in/ski-out listing available in Vail. It was an intensive project that took two years to complete.

The client did not want cliché ski house decor. Instead, she envisioned a style she described as "downhill racer"—clean, modern, and edgy. She had contracted K.H. Webb Architects of Vail to design a modern stone and glass home, and we all collaborated on the project from day one to create a seamless exterior and interior for our client. The architecture that Kyle Webb designed was soaring and dramatic. The interiors had to be powerful in their own right, while not competing with this strong architecture.

The home is a tour de force in the mere scale of its spaces, which are heightened by their dramatic views. These rooms were created not to impress, although they do, but to be truly enjoyed by family and friends. The colors in the house came out of the landscape: the spruce green of the evergreens in the surrounding forests and the white, tan, and brown barks of the Aspen trees. Everything in the house was designed for comfort, but with a rough organic quality inspired by nature, all infused with a modern edge that captures the spirit of this world-class ski resort.

Upon opening the front door, you encounter a long gallery with thirty-foot ceilings. We custom designed tiered iron chandeliers and a series of sconces for this grand entrance. The drama of this entry is all about mixing materials to create a timeless modern look. The stone, glass, stainless-steel, and forged-iron lighting create a dramatic yet classic entry.

Kyle Webb Architects of Vail designed a modern stone and glass house with dramatic views of the landscape.

The focal point of the entry is the stone fireplace. I knew I had to find a show-stopping light fixture to hang above it, and this stunning rock crystal chandelier that looked like it had been made from chunks of ice was perfect. To make it work in this vast ceiling, I scaled it up to four times its original size. The result is unexpected and dramatic.

The strong architecture and materials of this house required furnishings with great texture and scale. I needed to find furniture that felt natural and not "decorated" for this home. New ideas such as the leather benches instead of chairs around a breakfast table enhance the uniqueness of this home without distracting from the architecture. With classic furniture detailed with leather and textured wools and chenilles, this modern home will never feel dated.

The kitchen continues the sleek design with a mix of walnut cabinets, mica tile backsplash, nickel hardware, and stainless-steel countertop and appliances. At the island, bar stools in leather with open geometric backs complement the nearby benches at the breakfast nook. Benches and bar stools, instead of chairs, give a comfortable and fresh vibe to this space. Lighting is key, and the mirror and iron fixtures set the tone of the entire home.

In the family room (opposite), comfort is the main priority, but not at the expense of great design. A view of the Vail valley is accented by suede curtains with a green inset detail. The chairs swivel to accommodate TV viewing (or mountain gazing), and the Donghia table anchors the room with its sculptural shape. Chenille fabrics bring comfort, and the beautiful geometric-patterned rug is soft underfoot.

The sheer window treatments in the bathroom have twig patterns that look like the branches outside the window. The mix of stone and glass tiles with a sculptural tub makes this room as functional as it is beautiful but does not distract from the strong architecture of the space. The bed in the master bedroom was made from an Aspen tree (opposite). The branches were sawed in place to fit the vaulted ceiling.

For the master bath, I had nickel branch fixtures made to bring a bit of the outside in, but with a modern touch. The expansive shower has two showerheads and can be entered from both sides of the bathroom, with a bench for a steam shower. Everything is clean and sleek and perfectly matches the client's vision for her home.

The teenage daughter's bedroom is distinguished by the architectural lines of its soaring canopy bed. It has a mix of nail heads and leather, with a hint of crystal just to soften the room and add sparkle. The curtains are from France and have cutout snowflake designs along the hem's border.

On the lower level are the play spaces: the billiard room, a video wall with leather swivel chairs for video games, and a bar with hammered copper counter and swivel stools. Another lounge space for grownups is nearby, and all these spaces open up to the heated outdoor swimming pool.

OCEAN HOUSE RESORT SUITE
A Weekend Escape in a Landmark Hotel

Nestled on a beautiful bluff in Watch Hill, Rhode Island, stands the Ocean House, an old grande-dame hotel built in 1885 and painstakingly restored by a friend of mine from Greenwich, Connecticut.

The Ocean House is not just a landmark; it is the heart of the community and a place for families and friends to gather for memorable occasions in this quintessential New England summer village. People come to celebrate anniversaries, weddings, and the fourth of July, or just to enjoy weekend brunch.

I was fortunate enough to be asked by my friend to decorate the Tower Suite, a soaring triplex apartment at the very top of the hotel. The story goes that this grand space was originally the wedding suite. The restored suite was intended to be used as the VIP accommodations for the hotel, but the owner loved it so much that he bought it for himself and his family to keep for future gatherings.

The apartment is a unique architectural space; it feels like a tree fort, with its grand sculptural staircase up to the widow's walk (the signature peak of the hotel). I wanted to design a space that reflected the surrounding landscape

As you climb the stairs you find a cozy landing that doubles as a study with a day bed for extra guests.

of sea and sky. In the widow's walk one can look out peephole windows to panoramic views that stretch as far as Fishers Island, Stonington, Newport, Long Island, and miles and miles of the Atlantic Ocean. Naturally, the color scheme was looking me straight in the eye. I created a palette of blue, white, and sand, adding a hint of British Colonial mixed with a subtly nautical feel. I intended to give the apartment a timeless quality that would befit this landmark hotel's history.

On the main living space is a comfortable and inviting mix of upholstered, cane, and bamboo furniture. The windows were left unadorned so that nothing would compete with the views. Window seats were created for people to sit and gaze across the shoreline.

To emphasize that this is a place to come together and have fun, I added a game table and console that can double as a bar or serving place at cocktail hour.

The dining alcove has a custom curved banquette for eating. The blue glasses and carved ivory accessories are reminiscent of the whaling period, when this hotel was built.

The dark blue walls of the master bedroom are offset by a white lacquered bamboo canopy bed, with crisp blue and white embroidered bedding.

The refreshing color scheme of crisp blue and white continues into the master bath. I had Ocean House towels custom monogrammed to decorate the tub. A beach stone floor in the shower completes the relaxed, New England vacation vibe.

OUTDOOR ENTERTAINING
Making Outdoor Spaces an Extension of Your Home

When designing your home, don't forget to give your outdoor spaces the same attention that you apply to your indoor rooms. When I think about my exteriors I treat each area like a room: the outdoor kitchen (not just a grill), dining room (not just a table and chairs), or living room (not just a collection of outdoor seating). Your outdoor area can effectively extend the square footage of your home. The materials used today in all-weather rugs and furniture, plus outdoor fabrics for cushions, pillows, and draperies, can make your outdoor area a true extension of your indoor space.

My own outdoor living room was inspired by the wonderful way I feel when I travel in Europe. So I decided to bring that relaxed European atmosphere to my own Connecticut property, with a bocce court, grape vines over my pergola, outdoor fountains, and a Tuscan outdoor pizza oven. When the light goes down you would swear you were in Tuscany or Provence.

Bring your trays, throws, and candles outside and you'll immediately create an inviting and intimate feel for your terrace, porch, or gazebo. As much as I love outdoor elements in my interiors, such as lanterns and garden ornaments, I conversely enjoy using indoor pieces outside. Unexpected touches like lamps and curtains create instant ambience.

Blur the line between interior and exterior, and your home will feel more cohesive, plus you can relax among the sounds of fountains, the warmth of torches, and the beauty of natural gardens.

Make your terraces an extension of your home. An outdoor kitchen will get your family out of doors and enjoying your yard for a longer part of the year. Retractable awnings create an outdoor dining room and are as beautiful as they are functional.

Enhance your outdoor spaces with hurricane lanterns, wicker serving baskets, and flowers. These little features turn outdoor furniture into true living spaces. Pretty pillows, glassware, and linen add color, texture, and glamour to your entertaining.

I will find any excuse to add the sound of water to my outdoor spaces. Most people think of a garden as just flowers, but a koi pond, the texture of gravel, and stone urns and benches create outdoor serenity. I love a pergola or colonnade that directs your eye to another area of your garden.

Covered spaces, whether under a market umbrella or a great gazebo, draw you to the outdoors and offer a place to take in your beautiful lawn and surroundings.

While vacationing in Italy I fell in love with the lifestyle of cooking outside (I even added a bocce court to my yard). We use our pizza oven all year round. Friends call on Sunday to say, "Are you making pizza today?" and we gather together to prepare and cook the meal of the day. I have even cooked a Thanksgiving turkey outside. This grill has created many great memories for family and friends.

HOLIDAY TRADITIONS
Decorating Your House for Family Gatherings

The holiday season, more than any other, is a time to gather with family and make memories that will last a lifetime. There is nothing more fun and memorable for me than Christmas, which is the quintessential decorating holiday (especially to a professional decorator like myself). From the day after Thanksgiving until New Year's, Christmas is celebrated in every detail of my home, from the entry mailbox, to the front door, to the mantel—as well as outdoors.

Traditions are such an important part of the holiday season, and my own family continues to embrace our rituals. Since childhood, both my children have had their very own Christmas trees in their rooms. Each has a special Christmas box filled with their own ornaments that we have collected together on vacations and at holiday bazaars, even their own artwork and found objects, like a shell from a beach, or their first baby shoes. Every piece is meaningful and has its own special story.

Each evening ("if they had been good") they could close their eyes and select one ornament to hang on their tree. The memory of their trees and Christmas box is still very special to both my children. Sharing meaningful moments and creating heartwarming memories together is to me what home, family, and holidays are all about.

Even the other members of our family, my three golden retrievers, have their own tree filled with dog ornaments and ribbons with dog biscuits. This tree honors our wonderful pets.

I love the smell, lights, and greenery that Christmas brings into the house at a time when winter's gray has taken over the gardens. To bring life back into your property, decorate your mailbox, gates, window boxes, and planters with greenery, pinecones, and berries. Introduce Christmas to the outside as well as the inside. This really helps create beautiful memories that will live long after the Christmas season has passed.

Who needs sled dogs when you have three golden retrievers? Even the dogs are decorated with their Christmas scarves and leashes.

Always find an excuse to light your fireplaces. It creates instant warmth and an aura of comfort and enjoyment to any space, inside or out. I love candlelight in any room, which adds romance to a space.

Holidays are about creating memories. Swag your mailbox, your gate, your mantels. The effort you put in will result in memories that your family will have forever.

ACKNOWLEDGMENTS

I would like to thank all my clients, who have given me the ultimate compliment and pleasure of allowing me to design their homes and create the gorgeous interiors you have seen in this book. As I have said many times, a designer is only as good as her clients. I have been blessed with a wonderful and interesting group of clients whom I now am privileged to call friends.

I have to thank Tommy Hilfiger, whom I have known since we were both just starting out in our businesses. Tommy made my introduction to Rizzoli, leading to the publication of my two books. I also have had the pleasure of working on many amazing projects and family homes with Tommy over the past twenty years. I would like to sincerely thank you, Tommy, for your guidance, loyalty, and friendship to me and my son, Spencer. You deserve all your success because you are a gentleman and mentor for so many and you always inspire.

I can be creative and design beautiful homes, but nothing would become reality if not for my able assistants at Rinfret Ltd. I truly appreciate all you do to make these ideas become homes. You make it all happen, and I am sincerely grateful. I hope you love what you do as much as I do.

Thank you Elizabeth Ethridge McGann and Taylor Lagerloef for your encouragement, marketing, and P.R., and for staying on top of me to meet my deadlines. You have been such a huge help in making this book possible.

I especially want to thank my CFO, Jo Ann Zawalski. You have kept my books, my sanity, and my secrets over the past twelve years. Without you I could never do all that I do. You are the rock and have been so important in my life and business.

A sincere thanks to Raul and Maria Obando, who have kept my home, my children, my pets, and my life beautiful. I love you both for always being there and being an important part of our family at work and especially at home. Thank you always.

A special thanks to Alex Tart and Charles Miers at Rizzoli for all your knowledge and talent. You have made this experience a pleasure, as has my fabulous book designer Paul McKevitt.

Darling Michael Partenio, David McCaughan, and Stacy Kunstel, my photographers and stylist, who make everything look so gorgeous (including me, since I hate having my picture taken!). I always love working with you. You are blessed with such talent and an amazing eye.

Most important, the inspiration for everything: my children, Spencer and Taylor Stebbins. You have lived through the creative process that has been our lives. You are both so smart and talented and I am honored and blessed to have you as my family, along with all our darling pets. I have dragged you to museums and antique stores, traveled the world with you, and made you carry a sketchbook to document your memories rather than cameras. I hope I have taught you to "see." Together we have collected amazing life memories. Always be grateful and inspired.

Last, Basil Mavroleon, who has always made me feel special and loved. You are family.

May all my readers feel as blessed as I do. Family is what life is about. Nourish it by having a life well lived with your families and loved ones. I hope this book has given you inspiration.